Step-by-Step, Practical Recipes Soups & Starters: Contents

Soups

Soups are a simple and nutritious way of filling up on your 'five a day'. Packed with flavour, these dishes suit all tastes.

Starters

The perfect beginning to a large meal or suitable as a snack on their own, these starters are quick and easy to prepare.

FLAME TREE RECIPE BOOKS

FLAME TREE has been creating family-friendly, classic and beginner recipes for our bestselling cookbooks for over 20 years now. Our mission is to offer you a wide range of expert-tested dishes, while providing clear images of the final dish so that you can match it to your own results. We hope you enjoy this super selection of recipes – there are plenty more to try! Titles in this series include:

**Cupcakes • Slow Cooker • Curries
Soups & Starters • Baking & Breads
Cooking on a Budget • Winter Warmers
Party Cakes • Meat Eats • Party Food
Chocolate • Sweet Treats**

www.flametreepublishing.com

Creamy Chicken & Tofu Soup

INGREDIENTS

Serves 4–6

225 g/8 oz firm tofu, drained

3 tbsp groundnut oil

1 garlic clove, peeled and crushed

2.5 cm/1 inch piece root ginger,
  peeled and finely chopped

2.5 cm/1 inch piece fresh galangal,
  peeled and finely sliced (if available)

1 lemon grass stalk, bruised

¼ tsp ground turmeric

600 ml/1 pint chicken stock

600 ml/1 pint coconut milk

225 g/8 oz cauliflower, cut into
  tiny florets

1 medium carrot, peeled and cut into
  thin matchsticks

125 g/4 oz green beans, trimmed and
  cut in half

75 g/3 oz thin egg noodles

225 g/8 oz cooked chicken, shredded

salt and freshly ground black pepper

FOOD FACT

Tofu is a white curd made from soya beans. It originated in China and is made in a similar way to cheese.

1   Cut the tofu into 1 cm/½ inch cubes, then pat dry on absorbent kitchen paper.

2   Heat 1 tablespoon of the oil in a non-stick frying pan. Fry the tofu in two batches for 3–4 minutes or until golden brown. Remove, drain on absorbent kitchen paper and reserve.

3   Heat the remaining oil in a large saucepan. Add the garlic, ginger, galangal and lemon grass and cook for about 30 seconds. Stir in the turmeric, then pour in the stock and coconut milk and bring to the boil. Reduce the heat to a gentle simmer, add the cauliflower and carrots and simmer for 10 minutes. Add the green beans and simmer for a further 5 minutes.

4   Meanwhile, bring a large saucepan of lightly salted water to the boil. Add the noodles, turn off the heat, cover and leave to cook or cook according to the packet instructions.

5   Remove the lemon grass from the soup. Drain the noodles and stir into the soup with the chicken and browned tofu. Season to taste with salt and pepper, then simmer gently for 2–3 minutes or until heated through. Serve immediately in warmed soup bowls.

1

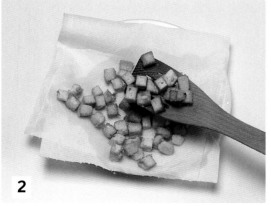

2

3

Thai Shellfish Soup

INGREDIENTS

Serves 4–6

350 g/12 oz raw prawns
350 g/12 oz firm white fish, such as
  monkfish, cod or haddock
175 g/6 oz small squid rings
1 tbsp lime juice
450 g/1 lb live mussels
400 ml/15 fl oz coconut milk
1 tbsp groundnut oil
2 tbsp Thai red curry paste
1 lemon grass stalk, bruised
3 kaffir lime leaves, finely shredded
2 tbsp Thai fish sauce
salt and freshly ground black pepper
fresh coriander leaves, to garnish

FOOD FACT

Sprinkling fish and seafood with lime juice improves its texture, as the acid in the juice firms up the flesh.

1 Peel the prawns. Using a sharp knife, remove the black vein along the back of the prawns. Pat dry with absorbent kitchen paper and reserve.

2 Skin the fish, pat dry and cut into 2.5 cm/1 inch chunks. Place in a bowl with the prawns and the squid rings. Sprinkle with the lime juice and reserve.

3 Scrub the mussels, removing their beards and any barnacles. Discard any mussels that are open, damaged or that do not close when tapped. Place in a large saucepan and add 150 ml/¼ pint of coconut milk.

4 Cover, bring to the boil, then simmer for 5 minutes, or until the mussels open, shaking the saucepan occasionally. Lift out the mussels, discarding any unopened ones, strain the liquid through a muslin-lined sieve and reserve.

5 Rinse and dry the saucepan. Heat the groundnut oil, add the curry paste and cook for 1 minute, stirring all the time. Add the lemon grass, lime leaves, fish sauce and pour in both the strained and the remaining coconut milk. Bring the contents of the saucepan to a very gentle simmer.

6 Add the fish mixture to the saucepan and simmer for 2–3 minutes or until just cooked. Stir in the mussels, with or without their shells as preferrred. Season to taste with salt and pepper, then garnish with coriander leaves. Ladle into warmed bowls and serve immediately.

2

3

4

Sweetcorn & Crab Soup

INGREDIENTS

Serves 4

450 g/1 lb fresh corn-on-the-cob
1.3 litres/2¼ pints chicken stock
2–3 spring onions, trimmed and
  finely chopped
1 cm/½ inch piece fresh root ginger,
  peeled and finely chopped
1 tbsp dry sherry or Chinese rice wine
2–3 tsp soy sauce
1 tsp soft light brown sugar
salt and freshly ground black pepper
2 tsp cornflour
225 g/8 oz white crabmeat,
  fresh or canned
1 medium egg white
1 tsp sesame oil
1–2 tbsp freshly chopped coriander

1 Wash the corns cobs and dry. Using a sharp knife and holding the corn cobs at an angle to the cutting board, cut down along the cobs to remove the kernels, then scrape the cobs to remove any excess milky residue. Put the kernels and the milky residue into a large wok.

2 Add the chicken stock to the wok and place over a high heat. Bring to the boil, stirring and pressing some of the kernels against the side of the wok to squeeze out the starch to help thicken the soup. Simmer for 15 minutes, stirring occasionally.

3 Add the spring onions, ginger, sherry or Chinese rice wine, soy sauce and brown sugar to the wok and season to taste with salt and pepper. Simmer for a further 5 minutes, stirring occasionally.

4 Blend the cornflour with 1 tablespoon of cold water to form a smooth paste and whisk into the soup. Return to the boil, then simmer over medium heat until thickened.

5 Add the crabmeat, stirring until blended. Beat the egg white with the sesame oil and stir into the soup in a slow steady stream, stirring constantly. Stir in the chopped coriander and serve immediately.

1

2

4

Chinese Leaf & Mushroom Soup

INGREDIENTS

Serves 4-6

450 g/1 lb Chinese leaves
25 g/1 oz dried Chinese
  (shiitake) mushrooms
1 tbsp vegetable oil
75 g/3 oz smoked streaky
  bacon, diced
2.5 cm/1 inch piece fresh root ginger,
  peeled and finely chopped
175 g/6 oz chestnut mushrooms,
  thinly sliced
1.1 litres/2 pints chicken stock
4–6 spring onions, trimmed and cut
  into short lengths
2 tbsp dry sherry or Chinese rice wine
salt and freshly ground black pepper
sesame oil for drizzling

1 Trim the stem ends of the Chinese leaves and cut in half lengthways. Remove the triangular core with a knife, then cut into 2.5 cm/1 inch slices and reserve.

2 Place the dried Chinese mushrooms in a bowl and pour over enough almost-boiling water to cover. Leave to stand for 20 minutes to soften, then gently lift out and squeeze out the liquid. Discard the stems and thinly slice the caps and reserve. Strain the liquid through a muslin-lined sieve or a coffee filter paper and reserve.

3 Heat a wok over a medium-high heat, add the oil and when hot add the bacon. Stir-fry for 3–4 minutes, or until crisp and golden, stirring frequently. Add the ginger and chestnut mushrooms and stir-fry for a further 2–3 minutes.

4 Add the chicken stock and bring to the boil, skimming off any fat and scum that rises to the surface. Add the spring onions, sherry or rice wine, Chinese leaves, sliced Chinese mushrooms and season to taste with salt and pepper. Pour in the reserved soaking liquid and reduce the heat to the lowest possible setting.

5 Simmer gently, covered, until all the vegetables are very tender; this will take about 10 minutes. Add a little water if the liquid has reduced too much. Spoon into soup bowls and drizzle with a little sesame oil. Serve immediately.

TASTY TIP

If Chinese leaves are not available, use Savoy cabbage.

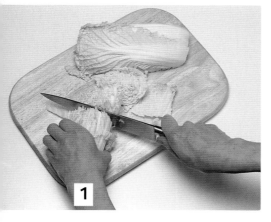
1

3

4

Vietnamese Beef & Rice Noodle Soup

INGREDIENTS

Serves 4-6

For the beef stock:
900 g/2 lb meaty beef bones
1 large onion, peeled and quartered
2 carrots, peeled and cut into chunks
2 celery stalks, trimmed and sliced
1 leek, washed and sliced into chunks
2 garlic cloves, unpeeled and
   lightly crushed
3 whole star anise
1 tsp black peppercorns

For the soup:
175 g/6 oz dried rice stick noodles
4–6 spring onions, trimmed and
   diagonally sliced
1 red chilli, deseeded and
   diagonally sliced
1 small bunch fresh coriander
1 small bunch fresh mint
350 g/12 oz fillet steak,
   very thinly sliced
salt and freshly ground black pepper

1 Place all the ingredients for the beef stock into a large stock pot or saucepan and cover with cold water. Bring to the boil and skim off any scum that rises to the surface. Reduce the heat and simmer gently, partially covered, for 2–3 hours, skimming occasionally.

2 Strain into a large bowl and leave to cool, then skim off the fat. Chill in the refrigerator and, when cold, remove any fat from the surface. Pour 1.7 litres/3 pints of the stock into a large wok and reserve.

3 Cover the noodles with warm water and leave for 3 minutes, or until just softened. Drain, then cut into 10 cm/4 inch lengths.

4 Arrange the spring onions and chilli on a serving platter or large plate. Strip the leaves from the coriander and mint and arrange them in piles on the plate.

5 Bring the stock in the wok to the boil over a high heat. Add the noodles and simmer for about 2 minutes, or until tender. Add the beef strips and simmer for about 1 minute. Season to taste with salt and pepper.

6 Ladle the soup with the noodles and beef strips into individual soup bowls and serve immediately with the plate of condiments handed around separately.

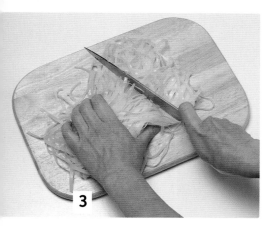

3

4

5

Rice Soup with Potato Sticks

INGREDIENTS

Serves 4

175 g/6 oz butter

1 tsp olive oil

1 large onion, peeled and
finely chopped

4 slices Parma ham, chopped

100 g/3½ oz Arborio rice

1.1 litres/2 pints chicken stock

350 g/12 oz frozen peas

salt and freshly ground black pepper

1 medium egg

125 g/4 oz self-raising flour

175 g/6 oz mashed potato

1 tbsp milk

1 tbsp poppy seeds

1 tbsp Parmesan cheese, finely grated

1 tbsp freshly chopped parsley

1 Preheat the oven to 190°C/375°F/Gas Mark 5. Heat 25 g/1 oz of the butter and the olive oil in a saucepan and cook the onion for 4–5 minutes until softened, then add the Parma ham and cook for about 1 minute. Stir in the rice, the stock and the peas. Season to taste with salt and pepper and simmer for 10–15 minutes, or until the rice is tender.

2 Beat the egg and 125 g/4 oz of the butter together until smooth, then beat in the flour, a pinch of salt and the potato. Work the ingredients together to form a soft, pliable dough, adding a little more flour if necessary.

3 Roll the dough out on a lightly floured surface into a rectangle 1 cm/ ½ inch thick and cut into 12 thin long sticks. Brush with milk and sprinkle on the poppy seeds. Place the sticks on a lightly oiled baking tray and bake in the preheated oven for 15 minutes, or until golden.

4 When the rice is cooked, stir the remaining butter and Parmesan cheese into the soup and sprinkle the chopped parsley over the top. Serve immediately with the warm potato sticks.

TASTY TIP

These potato sticks also make a delicious snack with drinks. Try sprinkling them with sesame seeds or grated cheese and allow to cool before serving.

1

2

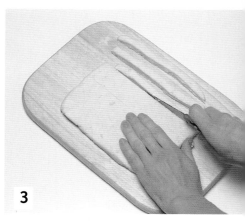

3

Rich Tomato Soup with Roasted Red Peppers

INGREDIENTS

Serves 4

2 tsp light olive oil

700 g/1½ lb red peppers, halved and deseeded

450 g/1 lb ripe plum tomatoes, halved

2 onions, unpeeled and quartered

4 garlic cloves, unpeeled

600 ml/1 pint chicken stock

salt and freshly ground black pepper

4 tbsp soured cream

1 tbsp freshly shredded basil

1 Preheat the oven to 200°C/400°F/Gas Mark 6. Lightly oil a roasting tin with 1 teaspoon of the olive oil. Place the peppers and tomatoes cut side down in the roasting tin with the onion quarters and the garlic cloves. Spoon over the remaining oil.

2 Bake in the preheated oven for 30 minutes, or until the skins on the peppers have started to blacken and blister. Allow the vegetables to cool for about 10 minutes, then remove the skins, stalks and seeds from the peppers. Peel away the skins from the tomatoes and onions and squeeze out the garlic.

3 Place the cooked vegetables into a blender or food processor and blend until smooth. Add the stock and blend again to form a smooth purée. Pour the puréed soup through a sieve, if a smooth soup is preferred, then pour into a saucepan. Bring to the boil, simmer gently for 2–3 minutes, and season to taste with salt and pepper. Serve hot with a swirl of soured cream and a sprinkling of shredded basil on the top.

HELPFUL HINT

To help remove the skins of the peppers more easily, remove them from the oven and put immediately into a plastic bag or a bowl covered with clingfilm. Leave until cool enough to handle then skin carefully.

1

2

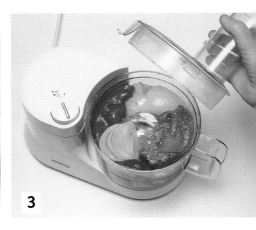

3

Rocket & Potato Soup with Garlic Croûtons

INGREDIENTS

Serves 4

700 g/1½ lb baby new potatoes
1.1 litres/2 pints chicken or
  vegetable stock
50 g/2 oz rocket leaves
125 g/4 oz thick white sliced bread
50 g/2 oz unsalted butter
1 tsp groundnut oil
2–4 garlic cloves, peeled
  and chopped
125 g/4 oz stale ciabatta bread, with
  the crusts removed
4 tbsp olive oil
salt and freshly ground black pepper
2 tbsp Parmesan cheese, finely grated

1 Place the potatoes in a large saucepan, cover with the stock and simmer gently for 10 minutes. Add the rocket leaves and simmer for a further 5–10 minutes, or until the potatoes are soft and the rocket has wilted.

2 Meanwhile, make the croûtons. Cut the thick, white sliced bread into small cubes and reserve. Heat the butter and groundnut oil in a small frying pan and cook the garlic for 1 minute, stirring well. Remove the garlic. Add the bread cubes to the butter and oil mixture in the frying pan and sauté, stirring continuously, until they are golden brown. Drain the croûtons on absorbent kitchen paper and reserve.

3 Cut the ciabatta bread into small dice and stir into the soup. Cover the saucepan and leave to stand for 10 minutes, or until the bread has absorbed a lot of the liquid.

4 Stir in the olive oil, season to taste with salt and pepper and serve at once with a few of the garlic croûtons scattered over the top and a little grated Parmesan cheese.

HELPFUL HINT

Rocket is now widely available in bags from most large supermarkets. If, however, you cannot get hold of it, replace it with an equal quantity of watercress or baby spinach leaves.

1

2

3

Classic Minestrone

INGREDIENTS

Serves 6–8

25 g/1 oz butter

3 tbsp olive oil

3 rashers streaky bacon

1 large onion, peeled

1 garlic clove, peeled

1 celery stick, trimmed

2 carrots, peeled

400 g can chopped tomatoes

1.1 litre/2 pints chicken stock

175 g/6 oz green cabbage,
  finely shredded

50 g/2 oz French beans,
  trimmed and halved

3 tbsp frozen petits pois

50 g/2 oz spaghetti, broken
  into short pieces

salt and freshly ground black pepper

Parmesan cheese shavings,
  to garnish

crusty bread, to serve

1   Heat the butter and olive oil together in a large saucepan. Chop the bacon and add to the saucepan. Cook for 3–4 minutes, then remove with a slotted spoon and reserve.

2   Finely chop the onion, garlic, celery and carrots and add to the saucepan, one ingredient at a time, stirring well after each addition. Cover and cook gently for 8–10 minutes, until the vegetables are softened.

3   Add the chopped tomatoes, with their juice and the stock, bring to the boil, then cover the saucepan with a lid, reduce the heat and simmer gently for about 20 minutes.

4   Stir in the cabbage, beans, peas and spaghetti pieces. Cover and simmer for a further 20 minutes, or until all the ingredients are tender. Season to taste with salt and pepper.

5   Return the cooked bacon to the saucepan and bring the soup to the boil. Serve the soup immediately with Parmesan cheese shavings sprinkled on the top and plenty of crusty bread to accompany it.

3

4

5

Lettuce Soup

INGREDIENTS

Serves 4

2 iceberg lettuces, quartered with
  hard core removed
1 tbsp olive oil
50 g/2 oz butter
125 g/4 oz spring onions, trimmed
  and chopped
1 tbsp freshly chopped parsley
1 tbsp plain flour
600 ml/1 pint chicken stock
salt and freshly ground black pepper
150 ml/ ¼ pint single cream
¼ tsp cayenne pepper, to taste
thick slices of stale ciabatta bread
sprig of parsley, to garnish

1 Bring a large saucepan of water to the boil and blanch the lettuce leaves for 3 minutes. Drain and dry thoroughly on absorbent kitchen paper. Then shred with a sharp knife.

2 Heat the oil and butter in a clean saucepan and add the lettuce, spring onions and parsley and cook together for 3–4 minutes, or until very soft.

3 Stir in the flour and cook for 1 minute, then gradually pour in the stock, stirring throughout. Bring to the boil and season to taste with salt and pepper. Reduce the heat, cover and simmer gently for 10–15 minutes, or until soft.

4 Allow the soup to cool slightly, then either sieve or purée in a blender. Alternatively, leave the soup chunky. Stir in the cream, add more seasoning to taste, if liked, then add the cayenne pepper.

5 Arrange the slices of ciabatta bread in a large soup dish or in individual bowls and pour the soup over the bread. Garnish with sprigs of parsley and serve immediately.

HELPFUL HINT

Do not prepare the lettuce too far in advance. Iceberg lettuce has a tendency to discolour when sliced, which may in turn discolour the soup.

2

3

4

Cream of Pumpkin Soup

INGREDIENTS

Serves 4

900 g/2 lb pumpkin flesh (after
  peeling and discarding the seeds)
4 tbsp olive oil
1 large onion, peeled
1 leek, trimmed
1 carrot, peeled
2 celery sticks
4 garlic cloves, peeled and crushed
1.7 litres/3 pints water
salt and freshly ground black pepper
¼ tsp freshly grated nutmeg
150 ml/ ¼ pint single cream
¼ tsp cayenne pepper
warm herby bread, to serve

1 Cut the skinned and de-seeded pumpkin flesh into 2.5 cm/1 inch cubes. Heat the olive oil in a large saucepan and cook the pumpkin for 2–3 minutes, coating it completely with oil. Chop the onion and leek finely and cut the carrot and celery into small dice.

2 Add the vegetables to the saucepan with the garlic and cook, stirring for 5 minutes, or until they have begun to soften. Cover the vegetables with the water and bring to the boil. Season with plenty of salt and pepper and the nutmeg, cover and simmer for 15–20 minutes, or until all of the vegetables are tender.

3 When the vegetables are tender, remove from the heat, cool slightly then pour into a food processor or blender. Liquidise to form a smooth purée then pass through a sieve back into the saucepan.

4 Adjust the seasoning to taste and add all but 2 tablespoons of the cream and enough water to obtain the correct consistency. Bring the soup to boiling point, add the cayenne pepper and serve immediately swirled with cream and warm herby bread.

TASTY TIP

If you cannot find pumpkin, try replacing it with squash. Butternut, acorn or turban squash would all make suitable substitutes. Avoid spaghetti squash which is not firm-fleshed when cooked.

Lettuce Soup

INGREDIENTS

Serves 4

2 iceberg lettuces, quartered with
  hard core removed
1 tbsp olive oil
50 g/2 oz butter
125 g/4 oz spring onions, trimmed
  and chopped
1 tbsp freshly chopped parsley
1 tbsp plain flour
600 ml/1 pint chicken stock
salt and freshly ground black pepper
150 ml/ ¼ pint single cream
¼ tsp cayenne pepper, to taste
thick slices of stale ciabatta bread
sprig of parsley, to garnish

1 Bring a large saucepan of water to the boil and blanch the lettuce leaves for 3 minutes. Drain and dry thoroughly on absorbent kitchen paper. Then shred with a sharp knife.

2 Heat the oil and butter in a clean saucepan and add the lettuce, spring onions and parsley and cook together for 3–4 minutes, or until very soft.

3 Stir in the flour and cook for 1 minute, then gradually pour in the stock, stirring throughout. Bring to the boil and season to taste with salt and pepper. Reduce the heat, cover and simmer gently for 10–15 minutes, or until soft.

4 Allow the soup to cool slightly, then either sieve or purée in a blender. Alternatively, leave the soup chunky. Stir in the cream, add more seasoning to taste, if liked, then add the cayenne pepper.

5 Arrange the slices of ciabatta bread in a large soup dish or in individual bowls and pour the soup over the bread. Garnish with sprigs of parsley and serve immediately.

HELPFUL HINT

Do not prepare the lettuce too far in advance. Iceberg lettuce has a tendency to discolour when sliced, which may in turn discolour the soup.

2

3

4

Mushroom & Red Wine Pâté

INGREDIENTS

Serves 4

3 large slices of white bread,
  crusts removed
2 tsp oil
1 small onion, peeled and
  finely chopped
1 garlic clove, peeled and crushed
350 g/12 oz button mushrooms,
  wiped and finely chopped
150 ml/ ¼ pint red wine
½ tsp dried mixed herbs
1 tbsp freshly chopped parsley
salt and freshly ground black pepper
2 tbsp cream cheese

To serve:
finely chopped cucumber
finely chopped tomato

TASTY TIP

This pâté is also delicious served as a bruschetta topping. Toast slices of ciabatta, generously spread the pâté on top and garnish with a little rocket.

1 Preheat the oven to 180°C/350°F/Gas Mark 4. Cut the bread in half diagonally. Place the bread triangles on a baking tray and cook for 10 minutes.

2 Remove from the oven and split each bread triangle in half to make 12 triangles and return to the oven until golden and crisp. Leave to cool on a wire rack.

3 Heat the oil in a saucepan and gently cook the onion and garlic until transparent.

4 Add the mushrooms and cook, stirring for 3–4 minutes or until the mushroom juices start to run.

5 Stir the wine and herbs into the mushroom mixture and bring to the boil. Reduce the heat and simmer uncovered until all the liquid is absorbed.

6 Remove from the heat and season to taste with salt and pepper. Leave to cool.

7 When cold, beat in the soft cream cheese and adjust the seasoning. Place in a small clean bowl and chill until required. Serve the toast triangles with the cucumber and tomato.

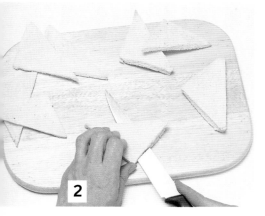

2

5

7

Thai Fish Cakes

INGREDIENTS

Serves 4

1 red chilli, deseeded and
   roughly chopped
4 tbsp roughly chopped
   fresh coriander
1 garlic clove, peeled and crushed
2 spring onions, trimmed and
   roughly chopped
1 lemon grass, outer leaves discarded
   and roughly chopped
75 g/3 oz prawns, thawed if frozen
275 g/10 oz cod fillet, skinned, pin
   bones removed and cubed
salt and freshly ground black pepper
sweet chilli dipping sauce, to serve

TASTY TIP

A horseradish accompaniment could be used in place of the sweet chilli sauce if a creamier dip is preferred. Mix together 2 tablespoons of grated horseradish (from a jar) with 3 tablespoons each of Greek yogurt and mayonnaise. Add 3 finely chopped spring onions, a squeeze of lime and salt and pepper to taste.

1 Preheat the oven to 190°C/375°F/Gas Mark 5. Place the chilli, coriander, garlic, spring onions and lemon grass in a food processor and blend together.

2 Pat the prawns and cod dry with kitchen paper.

3 Add to the food processor and blend until the mixture is roughly chopped.

4 Season to taste with salt and pepper and blend to mix.

5 Dampen your hands, then shape heaped tablespoons of the mixture into 12 little patties.

6 Place the patties on a lightly oiled baking sheet and cook in the preheated oven for 12–15 minutes or until piping hot and cooked through. Turn the patties over halfway through the cooking time.

7 Serve the fish cakes immediately with the sweet chilli sauce for dipping.

1

2

5

Hoisin Chicken Pancakes

INGREDIENTS

Serves 4

3 tbsp hoisin sauce
1 garlic clove, peeled and crushed
2.5 cm/1 inch piece root ginger,
   peeled and finely grated
1 tbsp soy sauce
1 tsp sesame oil
salt and freshly ground black pepper
4 skinless chicken thighs
½ cucumber, peeled (optional)
12 bought Chinese pancakes
6 spring onions, trimmed and cut
   lengthways into fine shreds
sweet chilli dipping sauce, to serve

TASTY TIP

For those with wheat allergies or who want to make this tasty dish more substantial, stir-fry the spring onions and cucumber batons in a little groundnut oil. Add a carrot cut into batons and mix in the thinly sliced chicken and reserved marinade (as prepared in step 3). Serve with steamed rice – Thai fragrant rice is particularly good.

1 Preheat the oven to 190°C/375°F/Gas Mark 5. In a non-metallic bowl, mix the hoisin sauce with the garlic, ginger, soy sauce, sesame oil and seasoning.

2 Add the chicken thighs and turn to coat in the mixture. Cover loosely and leave in the refrigerator to marinate for 3–4 hours, turning the chicken from time to time.

3 Remove the chicken from the marinade and place in a roasting tin. Reserve the marinade. Bake in the preheated oven for 30 minutes basting occasionally with the marinade.

4 Cut the cucumber in half lengthways and remove the seeds by running a teaspoon down the middle to scoop them out. Cut into thin batons.

5 Place the pancakes in a steamer to warm or heat according to packet instructions. Thinly slice the hot chicken and arrange on a plate with the shredded spring onions, cucumber and pancakes.

6 Place a spoonful of the chicken in the middle of each warmed pancake and top with pieces of cucumber, spring onion, and a little dipping sauce. Roll up and serve immediately.

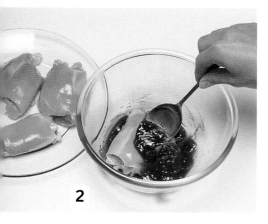

2

4

5

Hot Herby Mushrooms

INGREDIENTS

Serves 4

4 thin slices of white bread,
   crusts removed
125 g/4 oz chestnut mushrooms,
   wiped and sliced
125 g/4 oz oyster mushrooms, wiped
1 garlic clove, peeled and crushed
1 tsp Dijon mustard
300 ml/½ pint chicken stock
 salt and freshly ground black pepper
1 tbsp freshly chopped parsley
1 tbsp freshly snipped chives, plus
   extra to garnish
mixed salad leaves, to serve

FOOD FACT

Mushrooms are an extremely nutritious food, rich in vitamins and minerals, which help to boost our immune system. This recipe could be adapted to include shiitake mushrooms which studies have shown can significantly boost and protect the body's immune system and can go some way to boost the body's protection against cancer.

1 Preheat the oven to 180°C/350°F/Gas Mark 4. With a rolling pin, roll each piece of bread out as thinly as possible.

2 Press each piece of bread into a 10 cm/4 inch tartlet tin. Push each piece firmly down, then bake in the preheated oven for 20 minutes.

3 Place the mushrooms in a frying pan with the garlic, mustard and chicken stock and stir-fry over a moderate heat until the mushrooms are tender and the liquid is reduced by half.

4 Carefully remove the mushrooms from the frying pan with a slotted spoon and transfer to a heat-resistant dish. Cover with tinfoil and place in the bottom of the oven to keep the mushrooms warm.

5 Boil the remaining pan juices until reduced to a thick sauce. Season with salt and pepper.

6 Stir the parsley and the chives into the mushroom mixture.

7 Place one bread tartlet case on each plate and divide the mushroom mixture between them.

8 Spoon over the pan juices, garnish with the chives and serve immediately with mixed salad leaves.

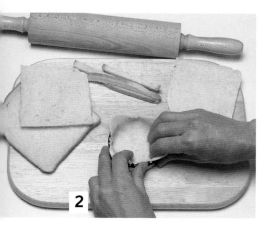
2

3

5

Coriander Chicken & Soy Sauce Cakes

INGREDIENTS

Serves 4

¼ cucumber, peeled

1 shallot, peeled and thinly sliced

6 radishes, trimmed and sliced

350 g/12 oz skinless boneless
   chicken thigh

4 tbsp roughly chopped
   fresh coriander

2 spring onions, trimmed and
   roughly chopped

1 red chilli, deseeded and chopped

finely grated rind of ½ lime

2 tbsp soy sauce

1 tbsp caster sugar

2 tbsp rice vinegar

1 red chilli, deseeded and finely sliced

freshly chopped coriander, to garnish

FOOD FACT

In this recipe, the chicken cakes can be altered so that half chicken and half lean pork is used. This alters the flavour of the dish and works really well if a small 2.5 cm/1 inch piece of fresh ginger is grated and added in step 4.

1 Preheat the oven to 190°C/375°F/Gas Mark 5. Halve the cucumber lengthwise, deseed and dice.

2 In a bowl, mix the shallot and radishes. Chill until ready to serve with the diced cucumber.

3 Place the chicken thighs in a food processor and blend until coarsely chopped.

4 Add the coriander and spring onions to the chicken with the chilli, lime rind and soy sauce. Blend again until mixed.

5 Using slightly damp hands, shape the chicken mixture into 12 small rounds.

6 Place the rounds on a lightly oiled baking tray and bake in the preheated for 15 minutes, until golden.

7 In a small pan heat the sugar with 2 tablespoons of water until dissolved. Simmer until syrupy.

8 Remove from the heat and allow to cool a little, then stir in the vinegar and chilli slices. Pour over the cucumber and the radish and shallot salad. Garnish with the chopped coriander and serve the chicken cakes with the salad immediately.

2

4

6

Roasted Aubergine Dip with Pitta Strips

INGREDIENTS

Serves 4

4 pitta breads
2 large aubergines
1 garlic clove, peeled
¼ tsp sesame oil
1 tbsp lemon juice
½ tsp ground cumin
salt and freshly ground black pepper
2 tbsp freshly chopped parsley
fresh salad leaves, to serve

1 Preheat the oven to 180°C/350°F/Gas Mark 4. On a chopping board cut the pitta breads into strips. Spread the bread in a single layer on to a large baking tray.

2 Cook in the preheated oven for 15 minutes until golden and crisp. Leave to cool on a wire cooling rack.

3 Trim the aubergines, rinse lightly and reserve. Heat a griddle pan until almost smoking. Cook the aubergines and garlic for about 15 minutes.

4 Turn the aubergines frequently, until very tender with wrinkled and charred skins. Remove from the heat. Leave to cool.

5 When the aubergines are cool enough to handle, cut in half and scoop out the cooked flesh and place in a food processor.

6 Squeeze the softened garlic flesh from the papery skin and add to the aubergine.

7 Blend the aubergine and garlic until smooth, then add the sesame oil, lemon juice and cumin and blend again to mix.

8 Season to taste with salt and pepper, stir in the parsley and serve with the pitta strips and mixed salad leaves.

3

6

7

Creamy Salmon with Dill in Filo Baskets

INGREDIENTS

Serves 4

1 bay leaf
6 black peppercorns
1 large sprig fresh parsley
175 g/6 oz salmon fillet
4 large sheets filo pastry
2 tsp sunflower oil
125 g/4 oz baby spinach leaves
8 tbsp fromage frais
2 tsp Dijon mustard
2 tbsp freshly chopped dill
salt and freshly ground black pepper

FOOD FACT

This is a highly nutritious dish combining calcium-rich salmon with vitamin and mineral-rich spinach. The fromage frais in this recipe can be substituted for live yogurt if you want to aid digestion and give the immune system a real boost.

1 Preheat the oven to 200°C/400°F/Gas Mark 6. Place the bay leaf, peppercorns, parsley and salmon in a frying pan and add enough water to barely cover the fish.

2 Bring to the boil, reduce the heat and poach the fish for 5 minutes until it flakes easily. Remove it from the pan. Reserve.

3 Brush each sheet of filo pastry lightly with the oil. Scrunch up the pastry to make a nest shape approximately 12.5 cm/5 inches in diameter.

4 Place on a lightly oiled baking sheet and cook in the preheated oven for 10 minutes until golden and crisp.

5 Blanch the spinach in a pan of lightly salted boiling water for 2 minutes. Drain thoroughly and keep warm.

6 Mix the fromage frais, mustard and dill together, then warm gently. Season to taste with salt and pepper. Divide the spinach between the filo pastry nests and flake the salmon on to the spinach.

7 Spoon the mustard and dill sauce over the filo baskets and serve immediately.

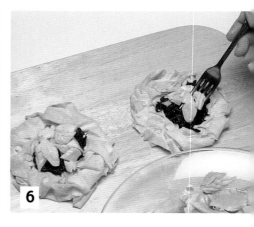

Sweet Potato Crisps with Mango Salsa

INGREDIENTS

Serves 6

For the salsa:

1 large mango, peeled, stoned and
   cut into small cubes
8 cherry tomatoes, quartered
½ cucumber, peeled if preferred and
   finely diced
1 red onion, peeled and
   finely chopped
pinch of sugar
1 red chilli, deseeded and
   finely chopped
2 tbsp rice vinegar
2 tbsp olive oil
grated rind and juice of 1 lime

450 g/1 lb sweet potatoes, peeled and
   thinly sliced
vegetable oil, for deep frying
sea salt
2 tbsp freshly chopped mint

1. To make the salsa, mix the mango with the tomatoes, cucumber and onion. Add the sugar, chilli, vinegar, oil and the lime rind and juice. Mix together thoroughly, cover and leave for 45–50 minutes.

2. Soak the potatoes in cold water for 40 minutes to remove as much of the excess starch as possible. Drain and dry thoroughly in a clean tea towel, or absorbent kitchen paper.

3. Heat the oil to 190°C/375°F in a deep fryer. When at the correct temperature, place half the potatoes in the frying basket, then carefully lower the potatoes into the hot oil and cook for 4–5 minutes, or until they are golden brown, shaking the basket every minute so that they do not stick together.

4. Drain the potato crisps on absorbent kitchen paper, sprinkle with sea salt and place under a preheated moderate grill for a few seconds to dry out. Repeat with the remaining potatoes. Stir the mint into the salsa and serve with the potato crisps.

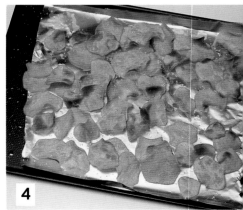

Stuffed Vine Leaves

INGREDIENTS

Serves 6–8

150 g/5 oz long-grain rice
225 g/8 oz fresh or preserved
   vine leaves
225 g/8 oz red onion, peeled and
   finely chopped
3 baby leeks, trimmed and
   finely sliced
25 g/1 oz freshly chopped parsley
25 g/1 oz freshly chopped mint
25 g/1 oz freshly chopped dill
150 ml/ ¼ pint extra virgin olive oil
salt and freshly ground black pepper
50 g/2 oz currants
50 g/2 oz ready-to-eat dried apricots,
   finely chopped
25 g/1 oz pine nuts
juice of 1 lemon
600–750 ml/1–1¼ pints boiling stock
lemon wedges or slices, to garnish
4 tbsp Greek yogurt, to serve

1   Soak the rice in cold water for 30 minutes. If using fresh vine leaves, blanch 5–6 leaves at a time in salted boiling water for a minute. Rinse and drain. If using preserved vine leaves, soak in tepid water for at least 20 minutes, drain, rinse and pat dry with absorbent kitchen paper.

2   Mix the onion and leeks with the herbs and half the oil. Add the drained rice, mix and season to taste with salt and pepper. Stir in the currants, apricots, pine nuts and lemon juice. Spoon 1 teaspoon of the filling at the stalk end of each leaf. Roll, tucking the side flaps into the centre to create a neat parcel; do not roll too tight. Continue until all the filling is used.

3   Layer half the remaining vine leaves over the base of a large frying pan. Pack the little parcels in the frying pan and cover with the remaining leaves.

4   Pour in enough stock to just cover the vine leaves, add a pinch of salt and bring to the boil. Reduce the heat, cover and simmer for 45–55 minutes, or until the rice is sticky and tender. Leave to stand for 10 minutes. Drain the stock. Garnish with lemon wedges and serve hot with the Greek yogurt.

2

2

3

Potato Skins

INGREDIENTS

Serves 4

4 large baking potatoes
2 tbsp olive oil
2 tsp paprika
125 g/4 oz pancetta, roughly chopped
6 tbsp double cream
125 g/4 oz Gorgonzola cheese
1 tbsp freshly chopped parsley

To serve:
mayonnaise
sweet chilli dipping sauce
tossed green salad

FOOD FACT

A popular, well-known Italian cheese, Gorgonzola was first made over 1,100 years ago in the village of the same name near Milan. Now mostly produced in Lombardy, it is made from pasteurised cows' milk and allowed to ripen for at least 3 months, giving it a rich but not overpowering flavour. Unlike most blue cheeses, it should have a greater concentration of veining towards the centre of the cheese.

1 Preheat the oven to 200°C/400°F/Gas Mark 6. Scrub the potatoes, then prick a few times with a fork or skewer and place directly on the top shelf of the oven. Bake in the preheated oven for at least 1 hour, or until tender. The potatoes are cooked when they yield gently to the pressure of your hand.

2 Set the potatoes aside until cool enough to handle, then cut in half and scoop the flesh into a bowl and reserve. Preheat the grill and line the grill rack with tinfoil.

3 Mix together the oil and the paprika and use half to brush the outside of the potato skins. Place on the grill rack under the preheated hot grill and cook for 5 minutes, or until crisp, turning as necessary.

4 Heat the remaining paprika-flavoured oil and gently fry the pancetta until crisp. Add to the potato flesh along with the cream, Gorgonzola cheese and parsley. Halve the potato skins and fill with the Gorgonzola filling. Return to the oven for a further 15 minutes to heat through. Sprinkle with a little more paprika and serve immediately with mayonnaise, sweet chilli sauce and a green salad.

2

3

4

Crispy Pork Wontons

INGREDIENTS

Serves 4

1 small onion, peeled and
   roughly chopped
2 garlic cloves, peeled and crushed
1 green chilli, deseeded and chopped
2.5 cm/1 inch piece fresh root ginger,
   peeled and roughly chopped
450 g/1 lb lean pork mince
4 tbsp freshly chopped coriander
1 tsp Chinese five spice powder
salt and freshly ground black pepper
20 wonton wrappers
1 medium egg, lightly beaten
vegetable oil for deep-frying
chilli sauce, to serve

HELPFUL HINT

When frying the wontons, use a deep, heavy-based saucepan or special deep-fat fryer. Never fill the pan more than one-third full with oil. To check the temperature, either use a cooking thermometer, or drop a cube of day-old bread into the hot oil. It will turn golden-brown in 45 seconds when the oil is hot enough.

1   Place the onion, garlic, chilli and ginger in a food processor and blend until very finely chopped. Add the pork, coriander and Chinese five spice powder. Season to taste with salt and pepper, then blend again briefly to mix.

2   Divide the mixture into 20 equal portions and with floured hands shape each into a walnut-sized ball.

3   Brush the edges of a wonton wrapper with beaten egg, place a pork ball in the centre, then bring the corners to the centre and pinch together to make a money bag. Repeat with the remaining pork balls and wrappers.

4   Pour sufficient oil into a heavy-based saucepan or deep-fat fryer so that it is one-third full and heat to 180°C/350°F. Deep-fry the wontons in three or four batches for 3–4 minutes, or until cooked through and golden and crisp. Drain on absorbent kitchen paper. Serve the crispy pork wontons immediately, allowing five per person, with some chilli sauce for dipping.

2

3

4

Mixed Satay Sticks

INGREDIENTS

Serves 4

12 large raw prawns
350 g/12 oz beef rump steak
1 tbsp lemon juice
1 garlic clove, peeled and
   crushed salt
2 tsp soft dark brown sugar
1 tsp ground cumin
1 tsp ground coriander
¼ tsp ground turmeric
1 tbsp groundnut oil
fresh coriander leaves, to garnish

For the spicy peanut sauce:

1 shallot, peeled and very
   finely chopped
1 tsp demerara sugar
50 g/2 oz creamed coconut, chopped
pinch of chilli powder
1 tbsp dark soy sauce
125 g/4 oz crunchy peanut butter

1 Preheat the grill on high just before required. Soak eight bamboo skewers in cold water for at least 30 minutes. Peel the prawns, leaving the tails on. Using a sharp knife, remove the black vein along the back of the prawns. Cut the beef into 1 cm/½ inch wide strips. Place the prawns and beef in separate bowls and sprinkle each with ½ tablespoon of the lemon juice.

2 Mix together the garlic, pinch of salt, sugar, cumin, coriander, turmeric and groundnut oil to make a paste. Lightly brush over the prawns and beef. Cover and place in the refrigerator to marinate for at least 30 minutes, but for longer if possible.

3 Meanwhile, make the sauce. Pour 125 ml/4 fl oz of water into a small saucepan, add the shallot and sugar and heat gently until the sugar has dissolved. Stir in the creamed coconut and chilli powder. When melted, remove from the heat and stir in the peanut butter. Leave to cool slightly, then spoon into a serving dish.

4 Thread three prawns each on to four skewers and divide the sliced beef between the remaining skewers.

5 Cook the skewers under the preheated grill for 4–5 minutes, turning occasionally. The prawns should be opaque and pink and the beef browned on the outside, but still pink in the centre. Transfer to warmed individual serving plates, garnish with a few fresh coriander leaves and serve immediately with the warm peanut sauce.

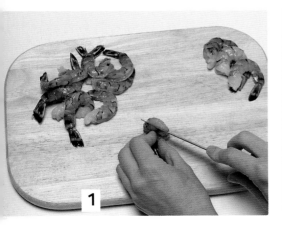

1

2

3

Step-by-Step, Practical Recipes Soups & Starters: Tips & Hints

Helpful Hint

Separate chopping boards should be used for raw and cooked meats, fish and vegetables. Currently, a variety of good-quality plastic boards come in various designs and colours. This makes differentiating easier, and the plastic has the added hygienic advantage of being washable at high temperatures in the dishwasher. If using the board for fish, first wash in cold water, then in hot to prevent odour. Also, remember that knives and utensils should always be cleaned thoroughly after use.

Food Fact

Rice noodles are fine, opaque noodles made from rice flour and are also called rice sticks. They originate from southern China, as rice is the primary growing grain in this area of the country.

Tasty Tip

Aromatics include onions, leeks, garlic, and often celery and carrots. Cooking them over low to medium heat in the pan before adding any liquid will help soften their texture and blend their flavours. Cook them by stirring occasionally, until they are soft but not browning, for about 5 minutes.

Tasty Tip

It is important to remember when making a soup to keep adding flavour even when the soup is served. By adding a bit of something fresh right at the end, such as fresh herbs, fresh citrus juice, a dollop or two of cream or yogurt, you will give your soup a hit of intense flavour and will highlight the deep, delicious, melded flavours in the rest of the soup.

Helpful Hint

When planning starters for a large group of people, remember that keeping the dishes basic will save on time, money and stress! For a varied yet simple menu, try Roasted Aubergine Dip with Pitta Strips (page 34), Sweet Potato Crisps with Mango Salsa (page 38), Stuffed Vine Leaves (page 40) and Mixed Satay Sticks (page 46). Many starters can be made ahead of time, and will then only require reheating when needed, allowing you to concentrate on larger dishes. If so, do make sure you have enough oven space to warm them and warming plates to maintain their temperature.

Helpful Hint

Seafood is an excellent addition to any starter menu, as it is usually quite quick to cook. But it is important to remember, when buying seafood, to buy from a reputable source that has a high turnover, to ensure freshness. Fish should have bright clear eyes, shiny skin and bright pink or red gills. The fish should feel stiff to the touch, with a slight smell of sea air and iodine. The flesh of fish steaks and fillets should be translucent with no signs of discoloration. Molluscs such as scallops, clams and mussels are sold fresh and still alive. Avoid any that are open or do not close when tapped lightly. In the same way, univalves such as cockles or winkles should withdraw back into their shells when prodded lightly. When choosing squid and octopus, they should have a firm flesh and pleasant sea smell.

Helpful Hint

Stock is so important when making tasty soups and it is easy to make your own! To make meat or vegetable stock, roast the vegetables and/or bones (and some cheap meat if you like) in some olive oil in an open pan in the oven, and then add all of them and the roasting pan bits to a basic broth or water along with some fresh herbs and spices. Simmer for 1–4 hours (less time if it is just vegetables, more if it includes meat) then strain out the chunks before using the stock to make the rest of the soup. Fresh chopped parsley added in the last few minutes of cooking adds a wonderful fresh flavour to soups.

Helpful Hint

If your recipe includes any pasta, then precook the pasta before adding it to the soup. This way any excess starch can be drained away and the pasta can be added last so it doesn't get overcooked. You can even use leftover pasta that you have stored in the fridge. Add the vegetables to your soup in the order of the time it takes to cook them: carrots, onions and potatoes first, then zucchini, fresh corn, frozen peas etc. during the last 10 minutes.

First published in 2013 by
FLAME TREE PUBLISHING LTD
Crabtree Hall, Crabtree Lane, Fulham,
London, SW6 6TY, United Kingdom
www.flametreepublishing.com

The CIP record for this book is available from the British Library • Printed in China

NOTE: Recipes using uncooked eggs should be avoided by infants, the elderly, pregnant women and anyone suffering from an illness.

18 17 16 15 14 13   10 9 8 7 6 5 4 3 2 1

ISBN: 978-0-85775-860-6

ACKNOWLEDGEMENTS: Authors: Catherine Atkinson, Juliet Barker, Gina Steer, Vicki Smallwood, Carol Tennant, Mari Mererid Williams, Elizabeth Wolf-Cohen and Simone Wright. Photography: Colin Bowling, Paul Forrester and Stephen Brayne. Home Economists and Stylists: Jacqueline Bellefontaine, Mandy Phipps, Vicki Smallwood and Penny Stephens. All props supplied by Barbara Stewart at Surfaces. Publisher and Creative Director: Nick Wells. Editorial: Catherine Taylor, Laura Bulbeck, Esme Chapman and Emma Chafer. Design and Production: Chris Herbert, Mike Spender and Helen Wall.